RYA Stability & Buoyancy

2nd Edition

© RYA Stability & Buoyancy
Copyright RYA 2009
First Published 2009

The Royal Yachting Association
RYA House, Ensign Way
Hamble, Southampton
Hampshire SO31 4YA

Tel: 0845 345 0400
Fax: 0845 345 0329
E-mail: publications@rya.org.uk
Web: www.rya.org.uk

ISBN 978-1-906-435-356 RYA Order Code G23

All rights reserved. No part of this publication may be stored in a retrieval system, or transmitted, in any form or by any means, electronic, mechanical, photocopying, recording or otherwise, without prior permission in writing from the publishers.

Stability and Buoyancy 2nd Edition
Technical Advisor: Andrew G. Blyth BSc, FRINA

A CIP record of this book is available from the British Library.
Ring 0845 345 0400 for a free copy of our Publications Catalogue.

Published by **The Royal Yachting Association**
RYA House, Ensign Way, Hamble,
Southampton SO31 4YA
Tel: 0845 345 0400
Fax: 0845 345 0329
Email: publications@rya.org.uk
Web: www.rya.org.uk

© 2009 Royal Yachting Association

All rights reserved.

Note: While all reasonable care has been taken in the preparation of this book, the publisher takes no responsibility for the use of the methods or products or contracts described in the book.

Illustrator: Pete Galvin
Cover design: Design House
Typeset: Jude Williams
Photo Credits: Paul Wyeth & Jeremy Evans
Proof reading and indexing: Alan Thatcher
Printed by: Sussex Litho

CONTENTS

	Introduction	4
1	**A word about...**	5
	Design Categories	5
	ISO 12217	5
2	**Buoyancy**	6
3	**Stability**	8
4	**Hazards common to most boats**	10
	Bad loading	10
	Filling with water	11
	Reduction of stability	11
	Resonant rolling	12
	Breaking waves	13
	Broaching in a following sea	14
	High speed handling	14
	Knockdown	14
5	**Characteristics of different boat types**	15
	Sailing dinghies and small sailing catamarans	15
	Sailing dayboats	16
	Offshore and coastal monohull sailing boats	17
	Offshore and coastal multihull sailing boats	19
	Runabouts, open launches and dinghies	20
	Offshore and coastal cabin motor boats	21
	High speed power boats	22
	Inflatables and RIBs	24
	Personal watercraft	26
	Inland waterways boats	27
6	**Annex A - More about stability**	28
7	**Annex B - Maximum safe heel angle**	34
8	**Glossary of terms**	35
9	**Further reading**	36
10	**Index**	37

INTRODUCTION

Going afloat will always involve certain dangers. No amount of planning and preparation can make even the best design of boat 100 per cent safe. If it did, boating would be a pretty dull sport. But good seamanship and a sound understanding of the area, environment, weather and of the boat itself will reduce the risks and help the skipper and crew cope with any potential hazards.

RYA Stability and Buoyancy examines the fundamentals of stability and buoyancy and applies these to offshore, inshore, coastal and inland craft, be it sail and power, big and small.

If you intend going afloat, be it sail, power, big or small, this book will give you the basic knowledge of the principles of stability and buoyancy, the related hazards that you may encounter and lists the Do's and Don'ts of the subject. Although too small to be exhaustive, this book nevertheless gives sufficient information to enable skippers to gain a good understanding of why boats float or sink, stay upright or capsize.

A WORD ABOUT... 1

Design Categories

As of 16 June 1998 every new pleasure boat of between 2.5m and 24m length when first placed on the market must be CE marked to show compliance with the Recreational Craft Directive (RCD) which requires that a boat satisfies the Essential Requirements according to one of four Design Categories. Design Categories are described primarily by the wave and wind conditions likely to be experienced and the circumstances under which such a boat might be used.

Design Category A - Ocean

Designed for extended voyages where conditions may exceed wind force 8 (Beaufort Scale) and significant wave heights of 4 metres and above, but excluding abnormal conditions.

Design Category B - Offshore

Designed for offshore voyages where conditions up to, and including, wind force 8 and significant wave heights up to, and including, 4 metres may be experienced.

Design Category C - Inshore

Designed for voyages in coastal waters, large bays, estuaries, lakes and rivers where conditions up to, and including, wind force 6 and significant wave heights up to, and including, 2 metres may be experienced.

Design Category D - Sheltered Waters

Designed for voyages on sheltered coastal waters, small bays, small lakes, rivers, and canals where conditions up to, and including, wind force 4 and significant wave heights up to, and including, 0.3 metres may be experienced with occasional waves of 0.5 metres maximum height for example from passing vessels.

So, if you are planning to buy or hire a boat, check which Design Category it has been given and whether or not this is suitable for your purposes.

The Design Category and Manufacturer's Maximum Recommended Load will be marked on the builder's plate. The boat may also display a RYA stability label which confirms that the RYA has assessed the boat type against the ISO Stability and Buoyancy Standard.

ISO 12217 - Small Craft Stability and Buoyancy Assessment and Categorization

The Essential Requirements of the RCD require (amongst other things) that a boat shall have stability, freeboard, and buoyancy characteristics appropriate to its Design Category. The RCD does not include detailed technical requirements, but relies on other, existing standards.

Because no universally accepted standard for assessing the stability and buoyancy of small craft was in existence at the launch of the RCD, one has been developed under the auspices of the International Standards Organization (ISO). It attempts to classify all types of boats, whether propelled by sail, engine or human power, and to assign a suitable Design Category.

While other methods of assessing stability and buoyancy are permitted, ISO 12217, developed internationally, has become the preferred approach.

Owner's Manual

The RCD requires that each new boat must be supplied with an owner's manual, which provides important operational and safety information. This often includes information relating to stability and buoyancy.

2 BUOYANCY

Buoyancy is the force generated when a volume of water is displaced by a solid body.

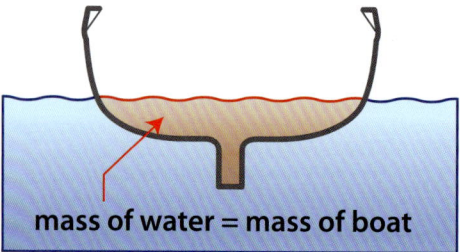

Fig 1

Archimedes demonstrated that the mass of water displaced by a freely floating solid object exactly equals the mass of that object *(Fig 1)*.

Wood floats because it has a density less than that of water. The mass is less than the available buoyancy.

A solid metal object sinks because it has a density greater than water. The mass exceeds the available buoyancy *(Fig 2)*.

Fig 2

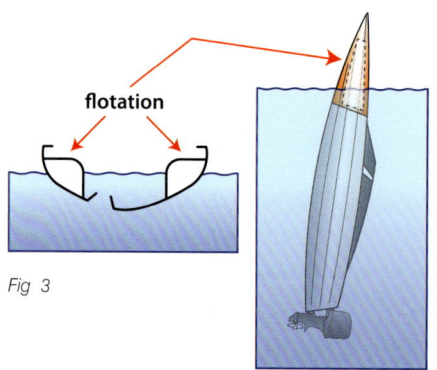

Fig 3

So, if the mass of a boat is less than the total volume of the material of a boat (its structure, ballast, engine and equipment) multiplied by the density of water it must always float, even if holed or completely filled with water *(Fig 3)*.

BUOYANCY 2

Boats with insufficient inherent buoyancy will float as long as the water is kept out of their interior. So even an open steel boat will float provided it has sufficient underwater volume to support its mass and enough freeboard to keep out the water *(Fig 4)*.

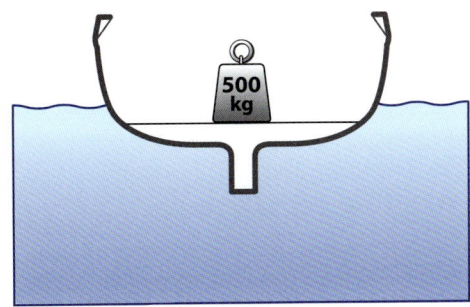

Fig 4

What are the buoyancy hazards?

The basic hazard related to buoyancy is that the boat might **SINK**.

Initially, this always involves the boat filling with water because of:

- Sudden swamping by waves, perhaps because of overloading or from the wash of another boat.
- Sudden swamping as a result of heeling to a large angle, perhaps because of an offset load or a strong wind.
- Slow swamping through submerged openings, hull damage or leaks through hull fittings.

It will then sink if it:

- Is not built of buoyant materials.
- Has insufficient flotation.
- Has leaky flotation tanks or water-sodden foam flotation.

3 STABILITY

A boat is said to be stable if it tends to return to the upright position after being disturbed by external forces – waves, wind or movement of the crew. The amount of energy trying to return the boat upright depends on three things:

- The mass of the boat *(Fig 1)*.

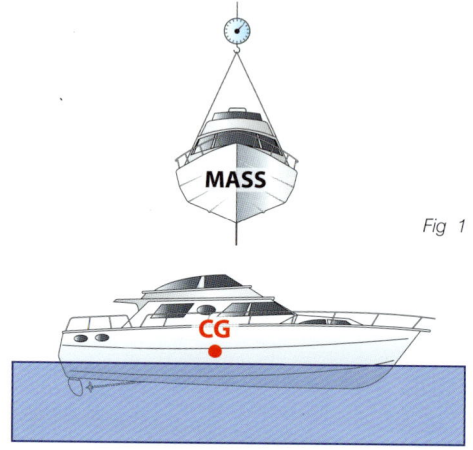

Fig 1

- The position of the Centre of Gravity (**CG**) *(Fig 2)* of all the elements making up the boat and its load (hull, masts, ballast, engines, fuel, stores, people, etc).

Fig 2

- The position of the centre of the volume of water displaced (Centre of Buoyancy - **CB**) *(Fig 3)* which depends on the shape of the immersed part of the hull. The **CB** will change with loading, heel angle and trim.

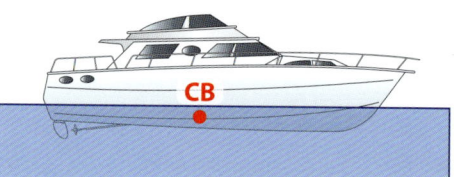

Fig 3

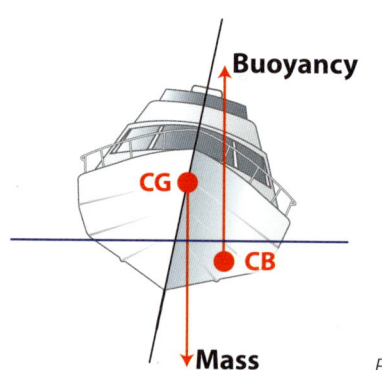

Fig 4

The boat is stable if, as it heels, the **CB** moves to one side more rapidly than the **CG** *(Fig 4)*.

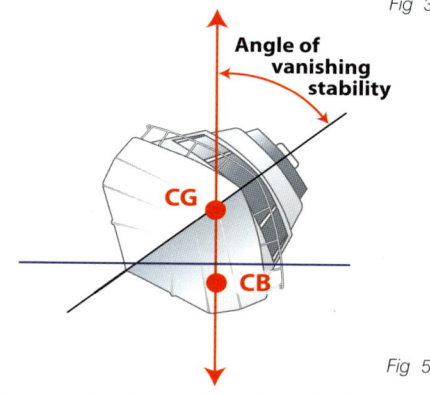

Fig 5

A boat may be stable when only heeled to small angles (say less than 30°) and unstable thereafter. The angle at which the boat will not return to the upright is called the: Angle of Vanishing Stability (**AVS**) *(Fig 5)*.

See Annex A: More About Stability.

STABILITY | 3

What are the stability hazards?
A boat must have sufficient stability to resist the forces to which it will be subjected. If not it will **CAPSIZE**. Causes of capsize include:

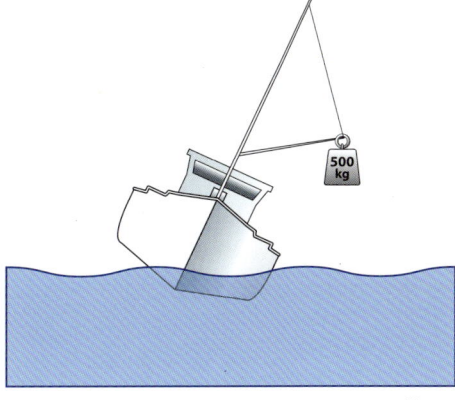

- Excessive offset load, e.g. crowding of people on board, heavy weights on one side *(Fig 6)*.

Fig 6

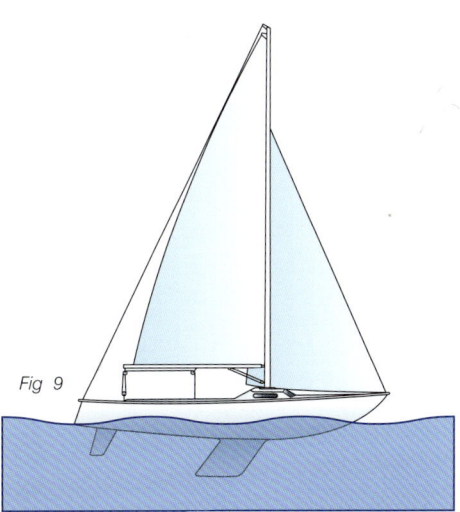

- Forces generated by waves, especially breaking waves *(Fig 7)*.

Fig 7

- Strong winds (this particularly applies to sailing boats) *(Fig 8)*.

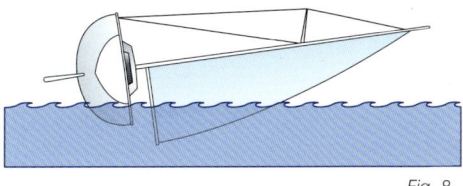

Fig 8

Fig 9

Fig 10

- Hydrodynamic effects (e.g. bad hull shape) *(Fig 9)*.

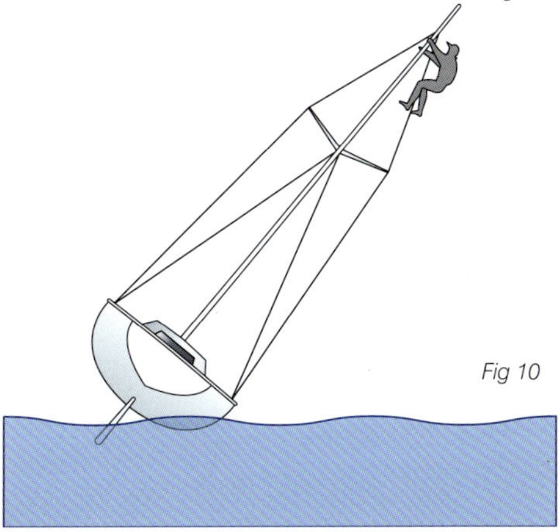

- Reduction in the original stability (e.g. extra weight added high up the structure) *(Fig 10)*.

9

4 HAZARDS COMMON TO MOST BOATS

Bad loading

Overloading is a common cause of sinking or capsize, especially in small boats or boats without decks. The load that can be safely carried depends on the conditions and whether or not the boat is fitted with any form of flotation.

DO NOT OVERLOAD THE BOAT.

Offset loading means the stability is less in one direction of heel making the boat more vulnerable to swamping. It will list, even in calm water and if the offset load is too great, the boat may capsize.

POSITION THE LOAD TO KEEP THE BOAT UPRIGHT.

Bad trim is caused by having the load too far forward or aft.

- Too far forward and the boat is difficult to steer and will ship water over the bow.
- Too far aft and it will be difficult to turn and may ship water over the stern.

TRIM THE BOAT BY SHIFTING THE LOAD.

Load too high reduces stability and makes capsize more likely. Putting the load low in the boat improves stability.

DON'T ADD LOAD HIGH UP IN THE BOAT.

HAZARDS COMMON TO MOST BOATS | 4

Filling with water

Swamping happens when an open boat or cockpit of a decked boat rapidly fills with water from above. This may be the result of bad loading and/or wave action. Depending on the extent of swamping and whether or not flotation is fitted, a boat being swamped may sink very suddenly.

KEEP WATER OUT.

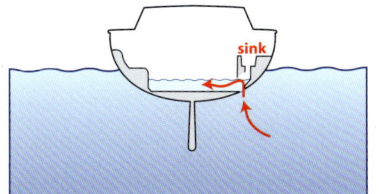

Flooding occurs when water gets into a boat slowly, for example when relatively small openings are submerged perhaps intermittently. It may also happen because of leaky or damaged hull fittings and pipework, via the toilet or sink.

CLOSE OPENINGS AND SEACOCKS AT SEA.

Reduction of stability

Extra topweight raises the overall **CG** of a boat and reduces stability. Fitting a radar antenna up the mast, or installing in-mast or headsail furling gear will inevitably reduce stability.

CHECK STABILITY IF ADDING TOPWEIGHT.

Loose water inside a boat (or on deck) has the same effect as extra topweight. As the boat heels, the water rushes to the low side exaggerating the heel – free-surface effect.

KEEP BILGES DRY AND AVOID WATER ACCUMULATING ON DECK.

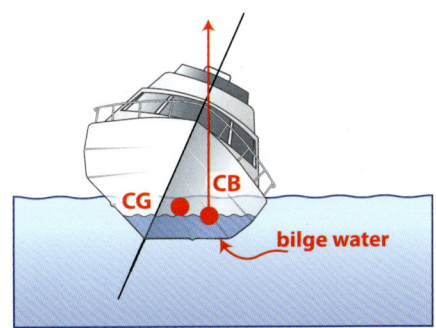

4 HAZARDS COMMON TO MOST BOATS

Hydrodynamic effects cause a reduction in the basic stability of some types of boat when travelling at high speed. Especially affects round bilge powerboats and broad, shallow draft monohull sailing boats.

KNOW YOUR BOAT AND ASK THE BUILDER.

Resonant rolling

Occurs when an initial disturbance causes a rolling motion which is progressively magnified by the action of wind or waves.

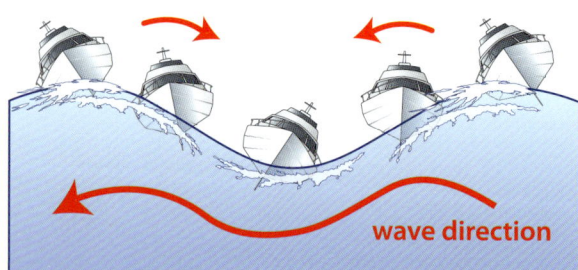

All monohulls can experience resonant rolling if encountering a series of fairly regular beam waves. The waves do not have to be large, but may simply have a period similar to the natural rolling period of the boat. Due to the damping effect of the sails, this is not normally of concern to sailing boats.

CHANGE HEADING TO AVOID BEAM WAVES.

Monohull sailing boats running dead before the wind, (even in smooth water), can develop a rolling action that may magnify so much that control is lost and the boat broaches violently.

SHEET IN THE MAINSAIL, OR RUN BY-THE-LEE WITH GYBE PREVENTER.

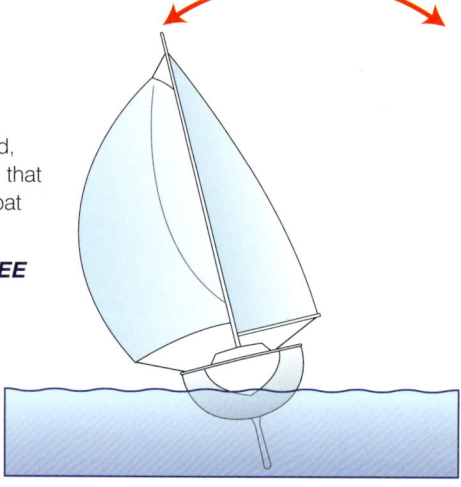

HAZARDS COMMON TO MOST BOATS | 4

Breaking waves

Waves are generated by the frictional effect of wind on the surface of the water. The stronger the wind, the longer it has blown and the greater the distance from shelter to windward (fetch), the bigger the waves.

Very steep waves are formed:

- When the wind strength is increasing rapidly.
- When wind and current are opposed (wind against tide).
- When waves are coming from different directions (e.g. after a sudden wind shift).

Waves break when they reach a critical steepness and gravity can no longer sustain their shape.

The graph below shows what significant wave height to expect but waves will quite often be nearly twice the significant height.

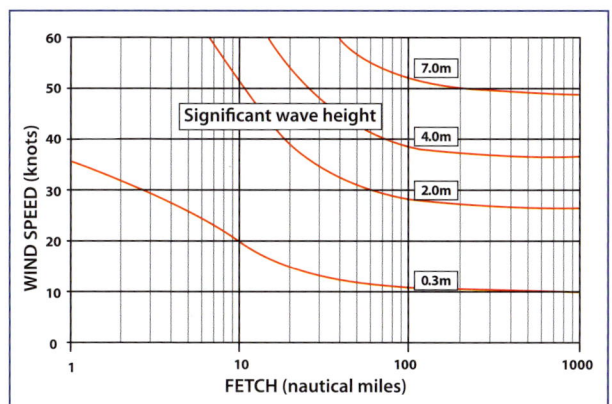

Breaking waves release large amounts of energy relative to their size. In many cases* this will be sufficient to knockdown and invert any boat under 24m length.

If unavoidable, do not take them beam-on, use a sea anchor if necessary.

WHERE POSSIBLE AVOID LARGE BREAKING WAVES*.

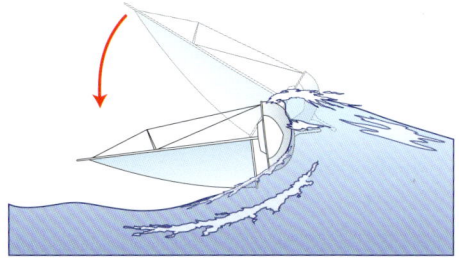 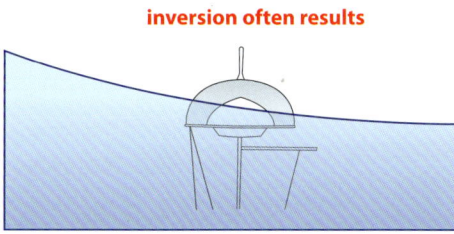

inversion often results

* See Annex A for more information on breaking waves.

4 HAZARDS COMMON TO MOST BOATS

Broaching in a following sea

This is the term used if, when running before large seas, a wave crest picks up the stern, causing the bow to dig in and the boat to slew through 90°. The violence of this uncontrolled manoeuvre results in the boat being thrown onto its side, sometimes becoming completely inverted.

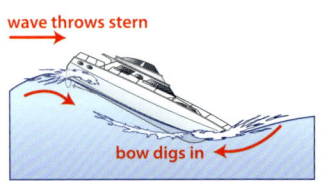
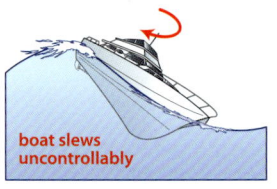
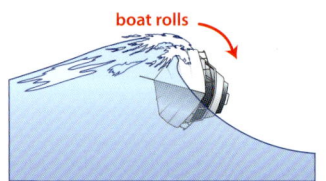

Traditional advice is to slow the boat by towing long loops of heavy warps or a strong drogue. Good helmsmen can often steer the boat away from threatening waves. This is a tiring task and requires frequent changes of helmsman.

CHANGE HEADING.

High speed handling

Fast boats, especially powerboats and multihulls (sail), can experience handling problems at high speed. These may result in dramatic swamping, sudden heeling, violent rolling, capsize or a combination of these.

KNOW YOUR CRAFT AND ASK THE BUILDER.

Knockdown

All types of sailing boats can be knocked down, (even in calm water), by a sudden strong gust of wind. With many dayboats and dinghies this will lead to filling with water and possible sinking. For most multihull and some dayboats this will lead to complete capsize and inversion.

BE ALERT IN GUSTY WEATHER, AND BE READY TO RELEASE THE SHEETS VERY QUICKLY.

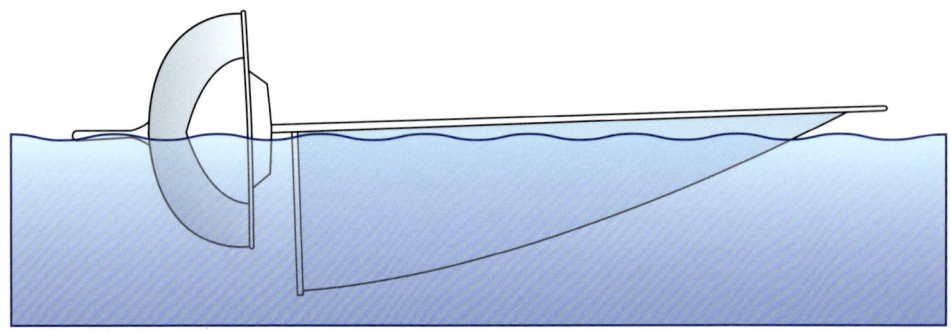

CHARACTERISTICS OF DIFFERENT BOAT TYPES | 5

Sailing dinghies and small sailing catamarans

Most dinghies and small sailing catamarans will, at some time, capsize. It's part of the fun. What is important is that they can be recovered.

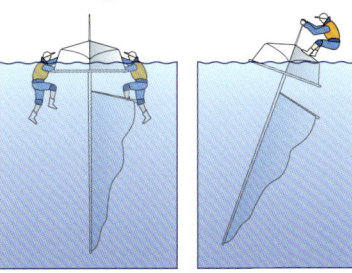

Principal hazards
- Knockdown, leading to inversion.
- Insufficient crew weight to right the boat.
- Swamping, (possibly due to overloading) leading to sinking.

Look for and know
- Minimum crew weight needed to recover after a knockdown or inversion.
- The means of flotation when in a swamped condition. This should be located in the sides and toward the top of the hull.
- The maximum number of crew for which swamped flotation is provided.
- When swamped, the boat floats so that it can be bailed out by one person.

DO
- ✔ Be alert, continuously shift your weight to counter-balance the wind.
- ✔ Make sure you know and practise the best way to recover after a capsize.
- ✔ Sail with enough crew to right the boat.
- ✔ Have a bailer of the appropriate size attached by a lanyard.
- ✔ Check your flotation tanks or foam, they may have taken on water.
- ✔ Check flotation bags are secure and fully inflated.

DON'T
- ✘ Carry more people for which there is flotation.
- ✘ Go out in conditions inappropriate for the boat's design.

5 CHARACTERISTICS OF DIFFERENT BOAT TYPES

Sailing dayboats

May suffer from a knockdown and swamping but should recover without sinking.

Principal hazards *(Fig 1)*
- Knockdown leading to swamping and possible sinking.
- Overloading resulting in swamping and possible sinking.

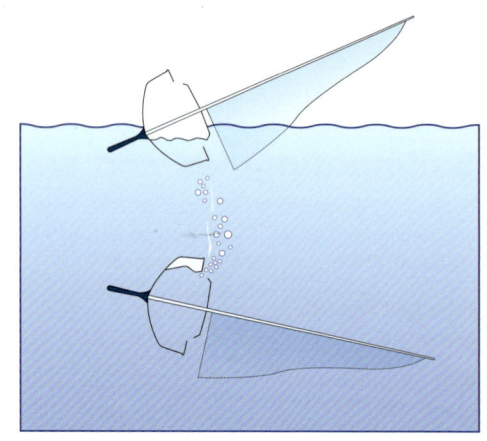

Fig 1

Look for and know *(Fig 2)*
- How to reef the mainsail
- Means of flotation when in a swamped condition. This should be located in the sides and towards the top of the hull.
- Maximum number of crew for which swamped flotation is provided.
- When swamped, that the boat floats and can be bailed by one person.

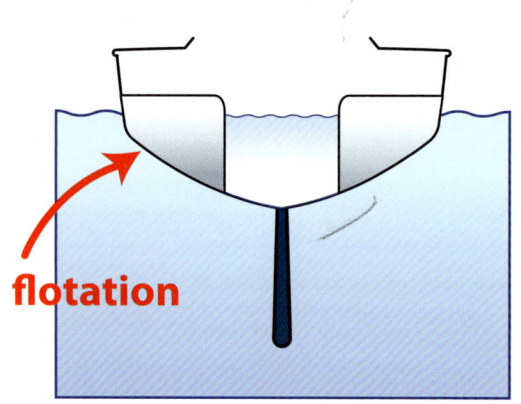

Fig 2

DO
- ✔ Be alert, and keep the mainsheet in your hand ready to release.
- ✔ Use crew weight to counter-balance the wind.
- ✔ Have appropriate size pump or bailer attached by a lanyard.
- ✔ Check flotation tanks or foam, they may have taken on water.
- ✔ Check that flotation bags are secure and fully inflated.
- ✔ Reef at the onset of rough weather.

DON'T
- ✘ Carry more people for which there is flotation.
- ✘ Go out in conditions inappropriate for the boat's design.

CHARACTERISTICS OF DIFFERENT BOAT TYPES | 5

Offshore and coastal monohull sailing boats

Inversion for prolonged periods is a major hazard. This should be avoided by good design.

Principal hazards
- At large heel angles, immersion of openings, resulting in loose water inside the boat (*Fig 4*).
- Knockdown by a gust leading to very rapid inversion.
- Breaking waves causing knockdown or inversion.
- Resonant rolling, leading to broaching.
- Broaching in a following sea.
- Reduction of stability due to extra topweight e.g. radar, roller furling sails.

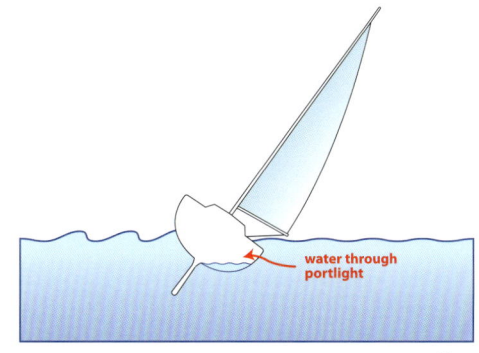

Fig 4

Look for and know
- All main hatches are near the centreline (*Fig 5*) and that these and other openings can be closed effectively.
- The cockpit will drain overboard quickly.
- Maximum steady heel angle to avoid downflooding in gusts (See Annex B for details).

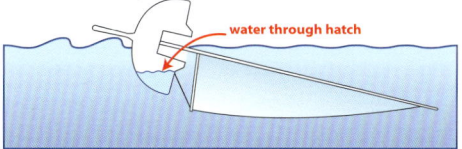

Fig 5

The Angle of Vanishing Stability is ideally more than:

	Over 12m loa	Under 12m loa
Category C	95°	105°
Category B	120°	130°
Category A	130°	140°

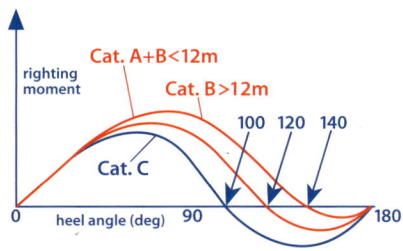

The area under the positive part of the Righting Moment Curve* is greater than the area under the negative part by a factor of about:

	Over 12m loa	Under 12m loa
Category C	1.25	2
Category B	4	6
Category A	6	8

- Extra topweight and additions aloft are included in the stability calculations.

* See Annex A for more information on righting moment curves

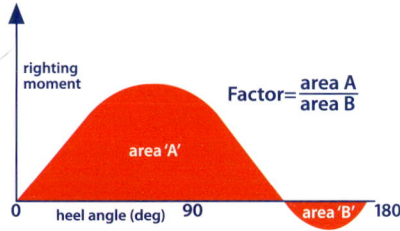

5 CHARACTERISTICS OF DIFFERENT BOAT TYPES

The following features will generally improve the ultimate stability of offshore and coastal monohull sailing boats:

- Increased physical length.
- Heavy displacement for size.
- High ballast ratio (upwards of 35%).
- High Angle of Vanishing Stability.
- High ratio of positive to negative areas under Righting Moment Curve.
- Good righting moment at 90° heel.
- Modest beam in relation to length.
- Good but not excessive freeboard.
- Minimal topside flare.
- Absence of large nearly flat areas of deck.
- Large heel angle before downflooding occurs.
- Increased keel profile area.
- Absence of bulwarks.

ISO Standard for Stability and Buoyancy

In developing ISO Standard for Stability and Buoyancy, the ISO committee agreed a formula for taking into account many of the above and other aspects affecting the stability properties of these types of boats. These include displacement in relation to length, topside flare, beam, downflooding angle and the wind speed at which downflooding is calculated to begin. This formula is known as STIX (Stability Index).

STIX is based on previous work undertaken by the Royal Ocean Racing Club on Triple S, later developed by the RYA as STOPS and currently used by the MCA Code of Practice for Small Commercial Vessels. STIX has been validated against a database of over fifty well known designs from six different countries.

Look for the following minimum STIX values:

Design Category	A	B	C	D
Minimum STIX	32	23	14	5

DO
- ✔ Close hatches and other openings at the onset of rough weather.
- ✔ Check for water inside and pump out before and during a passage.
- ✔ Be alert in gusty wind conditions, and reef before leaving sheltered water.
- ✔ Heave to, or run off streaming warps or a drogue in extreme conditions, to avoid being caught beam on to waves.
- ✔ Ensure hatch wash boards will not fall out if boat is knocked down or inverted.
- ✔ Ask the builder for stability information, including AVS, STIX and a Righting Moment Curve.

DON'T
- ✗ In rough weather, sail through known tidal rips, overfalls or areas where the bottom shoals rapidly.

CHARACTERISTICS OF DIFFERENT BOAT TYPES | 5

Offshore and coastal multihull sailing boats

Most large multihull sailing boats will not right after a capsize so it is imperative this is avoided.

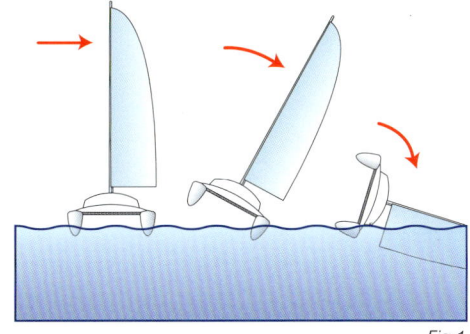

Principal hazards
- Knockdown by a gust leading to rapid inversion (*Fig 1*).
- Sudden heeling after turning from a following wind onto a reach, caused by the rapid increase in apparent wind strength, causing rapid inversion.

Fig 1

Fig 2

- Cartwheeling about the lee bow if pressed too hard on a reach leading to rapid inversion (*Fig 2*).

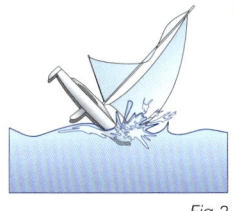

Fig 3

- Pitchpoling owing to carrying too much sail on a run leading to rapid inversion (*Fig 3*).
- Sinking after inversion owing to overloading or failure of flotation.

Look for and know
- Builder's information on what sail to set in different wind strengths.
- The cockpit will drain overboard quickly.
- How to escape from inside the boat after an inversion.

DO
✔ Know at what wind strength you should first reef.
✔ Be alert in gusty wind conditions, and reef before leaving sheltered water.
✔ How to release the sheets quickly.
✔ Close hatches and other openings at the onset of rough weather.
✔ Check for water inside and pump out before and during a passage.

DON'T
✘ Forget that the apparent wind will increase sharply when turning from a run to a reach.
✘ In rough weather sail through known tidal rips, overfalls or areas where the bottom shoals rapidly.
✘ Drive the boat hard when reaching or running, causing cartwheeling or pitchpoling.

5 CHARACTERISTICS OF DIFFERENT BOAT TYPES

Runabouts, open launches and dinghies
Also see the section on high speed power boats on page 22.

Fig 1

Principal hazards
- Swamping as a result of bad loading *(Fig 1)*, going too fast in waves or another boat's wash leading to possible sinking.
- Capsizing as a result of loose water in the boat or bad load distribution.
This includes passengers *(Fig 2)*, causing excessive heel.

Fig 2

Look for and know
- The maximum number of people for which the boat is suitable.
- The maximum recommended engine power as given in the owner's manual.

either
- The boat has good initial stability, is heavy and has a high freeboard.

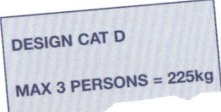
DESIGN CAT D
MAX 3 PERSONS = 225kg

or
- Has sufficient flotation fitted to stay afloat in a swamped condition. This should be located in the sides and toward the top of the hull.
and
- Maximum number of crew for which swamped flotation is provided.
and
- When swamped, the boat floats and can be bailed out by one person*.

DO
- ✔ Bail out the boat before use.
- ✔ Take care to load the boat properly.
- ✔ Carry less load when it is rough.
- ✔ Check your flotation tanks or foam, in case they have taken on water, check that flotation bags are secure and fully inflated.
- ✔ Have an appropriate size pump or bailer attached by a lanyard.

DON'T
- ✗ Overload the boat.
- ✗ Go out in conditions inappropriate for the design of boat.
- ✗ Go too fast astern, or astern into waves.

* ISO 12217 only requires minimal flotation to be fitted in non-sailing boats between 4.8m and 6m in length. A boat built down to this minimum would, if swamped, be impossible to bail out.

CHARACTERISTICS OF DIFFERENT BOAT TYPES | 5

Offshore and coastal cabin motor boats

Also see the section on high speed power boats on page 22.

Principal hazards
- Immersion of openings at large heel angles resulting in loose water inside the boat.
- Resonant rolling in beam seas, leading to capsize *(Fig 1)*.
- Broaching in a following sea.
- Knockdown by breaking waves, causing damage to windows and superstructure, can lead to inversion *(Fig 2)*.
- Reduction of stability caused by extra topweight e.g. radar.

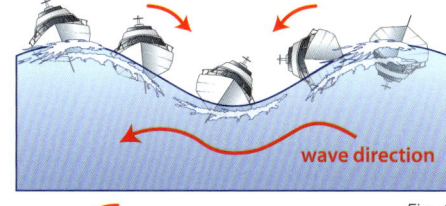

Fig 1

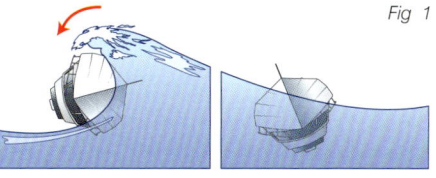

Fig 2

Look for and know
- Hatches and other openings can be closed effectively.
- The cockpit will drain overboard quickly *(Fig 3)*.
- The engine air inlet position is as high as practical *(Fig 4)* and fitted with water baffles or traps.
- Location of storm shutters for large windows (offshore only).
- All additions aloft are included in the stability calculations.

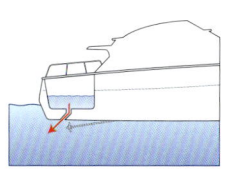

Fig 3   *Fig 4*

DO
✔ Close hatches and other openings at the onset of rough weather.
✔ Check for water inside and pump out before and during a passage.
✔ Ensure hatches and doors can be strongly secured.
✔ Secure deck gear and dinghies when going offshore.
✔ Fit storm covers over large windows at the onset of rough weather offshore.
✔ Heave to, or run off streaming warps or drogue in extreme conditions, to avoid being caught beam on to waves.
✔ Ask the builder for stability information, including a Righting Moment Curve.

DON'T
✘ In rough weather go through known tidal rips, overfalls or areas where the bottom shoals rapidly.
✘ Get caught beam-on to breaking waves.

5 CHARACTERISTICS OF DIFFERENT BOAT TYPES

High speed power boats

Also read the appropriate sections on power boats on pages 20 and 21.

Principal hazards

- Porpoising, the boat pitches continuously (even in calm water), sometimes quite violently.

- Chine-walking, above a certain speed the boat either sits on one chine or oscillates between both.

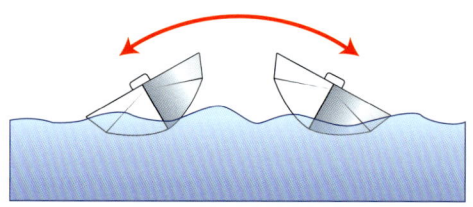

- Bow steering, the shape of the bow produces forces which cause the boat to sheer to one side. This is often accompanied by a violent roll.

- Bow diving, in following seas the bow digs into the wave ahead, resulting in a rapid deceleration, and sometimes almost complete submergence.

CHARACTERISTICS OF DIFFERENT BOAT TYPES | 5

- Fast tight turns produce high centrifugal forces which may cause the boat to heel outwards. Particularly applies to round bilge monohulls.
- Stability reduction at speed, making the boat less stable and more difficult to steer.

Look for and know

- About guidance on handling as detailed in owner's manual.
- That power trim or trim tabs are adjusted to give the correct running trim.

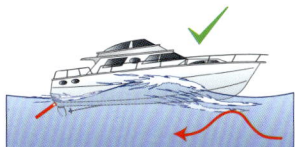

Trim tab down ensures the bow is down to face oncoming waves.

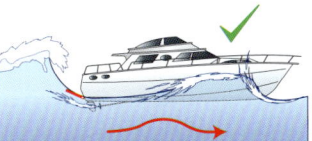

Trim tab up ensures that stern is down to maintain steerage and way.

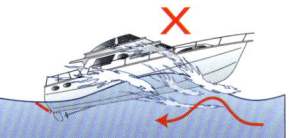

Trim tab up raises the bow and allows oncoming waves to come under the boat and reduce the effectiveness of steerage and increases the risk of possible rolling.

DO
- ✔ Get proper tuition in handling at speed.
- ✔ Read the waves, and use the throttle accordingly.
- ✔ Slow right down in busy or restricted waters or if people have to go on deck.
- ✔ Use trim controls according to whether it is a head or following sea.

DON'T
- ✘ Make needlessly sharp turns.
- ✘ Go too fast for the sea conditions.

5 CHARACTERISTICS OF DIFFERENT BOAT TYPES

Inflatables and RIBs

Also see the section on high speed power boats on page 22.

Principal hazards
- Swamping (*Fig 1*) as a result of going too fast in waves leading to possible sinking.
- Capsizing as a result of bad load distribution, including passengers, causing excessive heel.
- Flipping (*Fig 2*), bow over stern, through driving too hard into a head sea, wash or wind.

Fig 1

Fig 2

CHARACTERISTICS OF DIFFERENT BOAT TYPES | 5

Look for and know
- Maximum number of people for which the boat is suitable.
- Maximum recommended engine power as given in the owner's manual.
- The compartmentation of the inflatable tubes so that if one compartment is punctured the swamped boat will still float reasonably level.
- Self-bailers in the transom.

Check that all tubes are inflated in multiple tube types.

Fig 1

In single tube types a punctured tube is bad news!

Fig 2

DO
✔ Keep tubes firmly inflated.
✔ Take care to load the boat properly, keeping some weight forward to counterbalance the engine and helmsman.
✔ Carry less load when it is rough.
✔ Have the correct size pump or bailer attached by a lanyard.
✔ Check the inflated tubes and bottom compartments, they may have taken on water.

DON'T
✗ Overload the boat.
✗ Go out in conditions inappropriate for the design of boat.
✗ Go too fast astern, or astern into waves.

5 | CHARACTERISTICS OF DIFFERENT BOAT TYPES

Personal watercraft

Most personal water craft will capsize, it's part of the sport. However, it is important that they can be recovered without damage.

Principal hazards

- Capsizing due to waves or bad weight distribution.

- Sinking as a result of opening up the engine compartment while afloat.

Look for and know

- Maximum number of people for which the craft is suitable.
- Way to roll the craft when recovering after a capsize – avoiding possible engine damage.

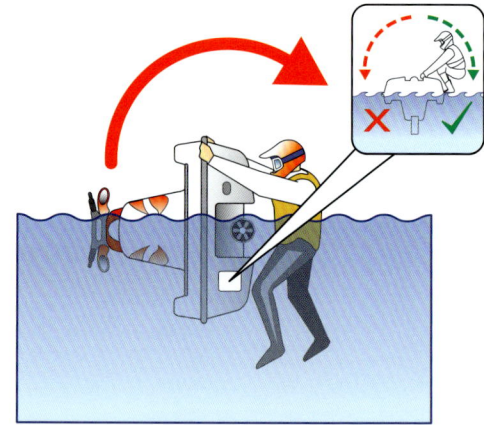

DO
✔ Check the flotation, in case the craft has taken on water.
✔ Know which way to roll the craft when recovering after a capsize.

DON'T
✗ Overload the craft.
✗ Go out in conditions unsuitable for the design of craft.
✗ Open the engine compartment at sea.

CHARACTERISTICS OF DIFFERENT BOAT TYPES | 5

Inland waterways boats

This section should be considered in addition to the appropriate section on the specific type of boat.

Principal hazards
- Immersion of openings at large heel angles, leading to loose water inside the boat.
- Getting 'hung up' on lock walls or sills *(Fig 1)*.

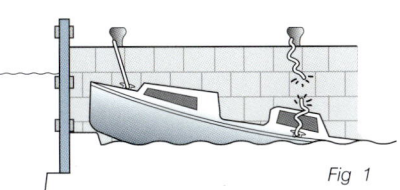

Fig 1

- Swamping as a result of wash from other boats, or bad positioning when a lock is being filled.
- Capsize due to bad load distribution or over-loading *(Fig 2)*.

Fig 2

Look for and know
- Wells and cockpits will drain overboard and not into the bilges *(Fig 3)*.
- Topside openings are high enough with respect to possible heel and trim angles.
- Maximum number of people for which the boat is suitable.

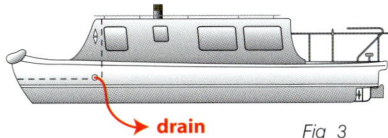

Fig 3

DO
✔ Keep the boat at a reasonable heel and trim by positioning the crew.
✔ Check for water inside the boat and pump out if necessary.
✔ Open lock paddles gently.

DON'T
✘ Overload the craft.
✘ Tie off your warps when descending in a lock.
✘ Moor too close to the upper set of lock gates.
✘ Get too close to weir streams.

6 ANNEX A - MORE ABOUT STABILITY

A boat is said to be stable when it has an inherent tendency to return to the original upright attitude after some influence has displaced it.

After being completely inverted, only a few boats are so stable that they will return to the upright without help. The extent to which they are positively stable is called the **RANGE OF POSITIVE STABILITY.**

The angle of heel beyond which (in calm water) a boat will invert rather than recover to the upright is called the **ANGLE OF VANISHING STABILITY.**

A boat is stable because the relative positions of the **CENTRE OF GRAVITY (CG)** and the **CENTRE OF BUOYANCY (CB)**, together with the weight of the boat, create a moment (force x distance) which returns the boat to the upright. The shortest distance between the line of the buoyancy force and that of the weight is called the **RIGHTING LEVER (GZ).**

This lever multiplied by the boat's weight becomes the **RIGHTING MOMENT (RM).**

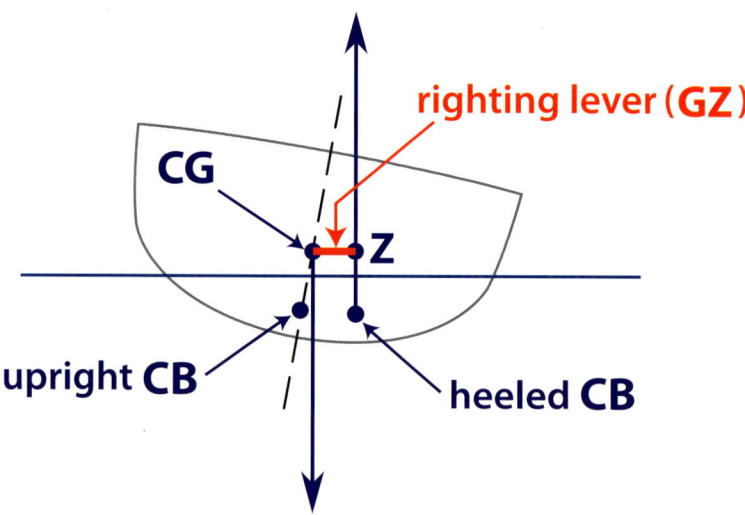

ANNEX A 6

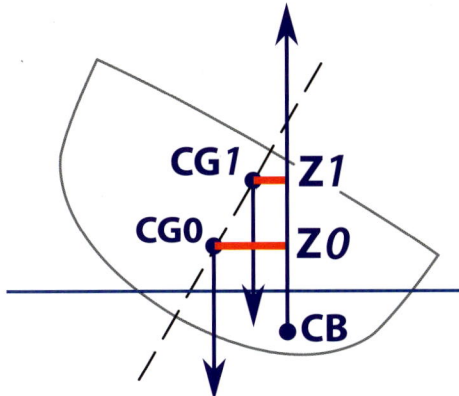

If the **CENTRE OF GRAVITY (CG)** is raised the stability will be reduced and if the **CG** is lowered the stability is increased. So weight added high up is potentially dangerous.

At small angles of heel, the stability is strongly affected by the shape of the part of the hull that is normally underwater (form stable).

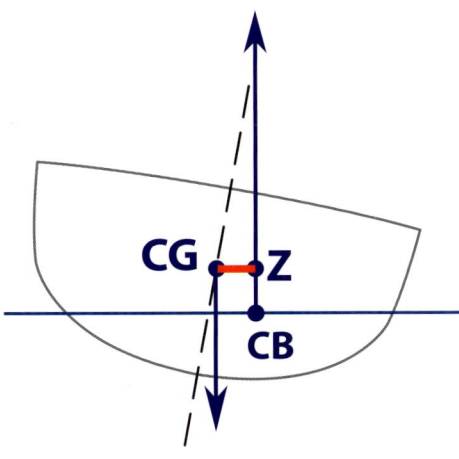

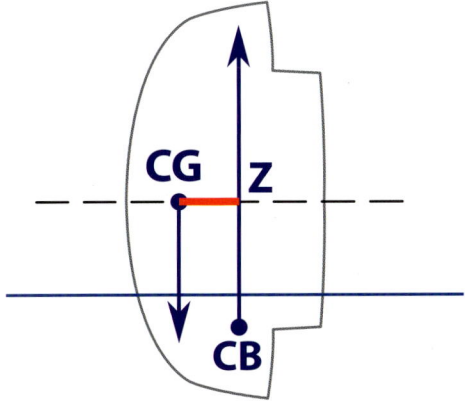

At larger angles of heel, the stability is strongly affected by the height of the topsides, the size of the superstructure and the volume of cockpit.

6 ANNEX A

The true position of the **CG** of a boat is found by conducting an **INCLINING EXPERIMENT** in which known weights are moved through known distances to apply a known heeling moment. By measuring the resulting angle of heel very accurately, and knowing the true weight of the boat, the position of the **CG** can be determined provided that the shape of the hull is known. Getting an accurate answer requires great care.

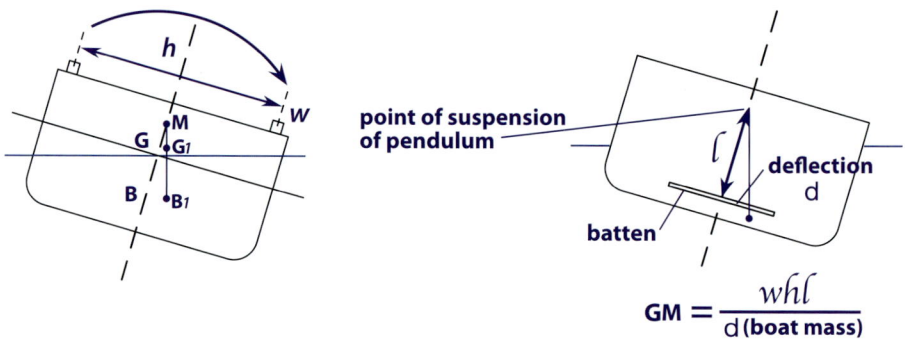

$$GM = \frac{whl}{d\,(\text{boat mass})}$$

Using a known position of the **CG** and a computer, it is possible to calculate the stability righting moment at any angle of heel. It is plotted as a graph of righting moment against heel angle. This is called the **RIGHTING MOMENT CURVE**.

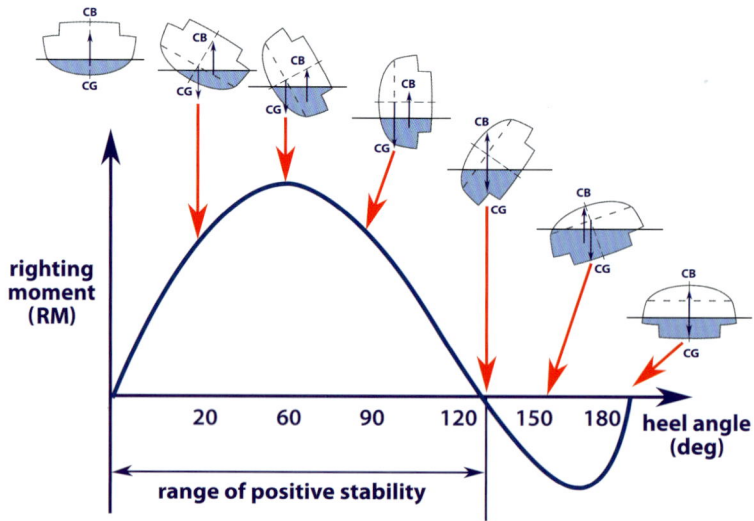

ANNEX A 6

For undecked boats where swamping is possible, the **RIGHTING MOMENT CURVE** has no meaning beyond the angle at which swamping starts.

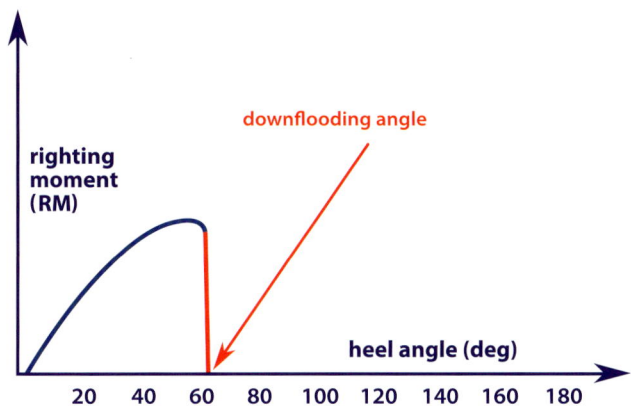

For most motor boats, the part of the **RIGHTING MOMENT CURVE** up to about 40° heel is the most important. However motor boats intended for very rough weather (like RNLI lifeboats) can be designed to be self-righting, by having very strong, watertight superstructures, so that the **RIGHTING MOMENT** is positive at all angles of heel.

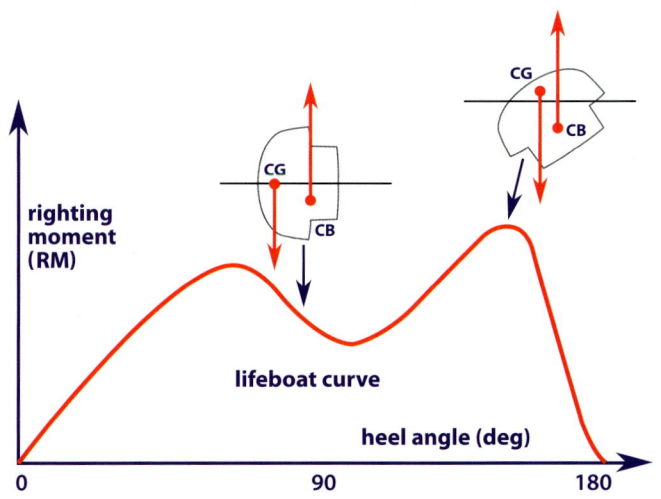

6 ANNEX A

For monohull sailing yachts in coastal waters (Design Category C) it is very desirable that the boat should recover from a knockdown. To do this, the **ANGLE OF VANISHING STABILITY** must exceed about 100°.

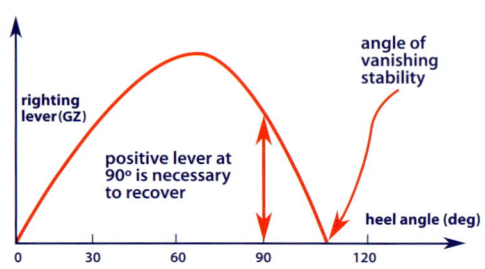

Monohull offshore sailing yachts (Design Categories A and B) risk being struck by very powerful breaking waves. For such boats a large **ANGLE OF VANISHING STABILITY** is required. Boats hit by a breaking wave with a height greater than the beam of the yacht are liable to be completely inverted.

The time taken to recover from an inversion is least when the **ANGLE OF VANISHING STABILITY** is closest to 180°, because then only a comparatively small amount of wave energy is needed to start the righting process.

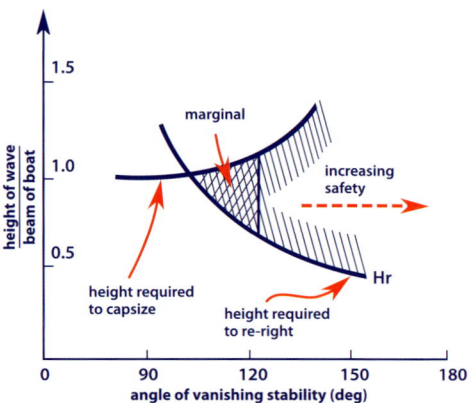

Another measure of the readiness to right after inversion is the ratio between the positive area and the negative area under the righting moment curve.

The smaller area B, the better the re-righting.

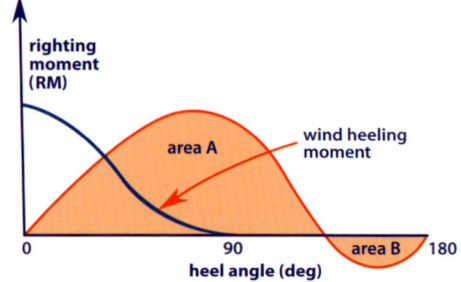

ANNEX A 6

Multihull sailing yachts have very different stability characteristics from most monohulls, because:

- The initial stability is much higher, so that the boat sails almost upright.
- The righting moment reaches a maximum at only 10° to 15° heel.
- The **ANGLE OF VANISHING STABILITY** is often less than 90°.
- The wind heeling moment does not decrease to very little at 90° heel.

Once the boat is heeled past the angle of maximum righting moment, complete inversion is virtually inevitable, and this will happen very quickly.

The safety of these craft is based on two principles:

1. providing information about which sails should be used in what wind strength and other guidance to help the user minimise the risk of inversion.
2. ensuring that if a multihull does invert:
   (a) the boat has sufficient flotation to ensure it does not sink, and
   (b) there is a means of escape for anyone trapped inside the boat.

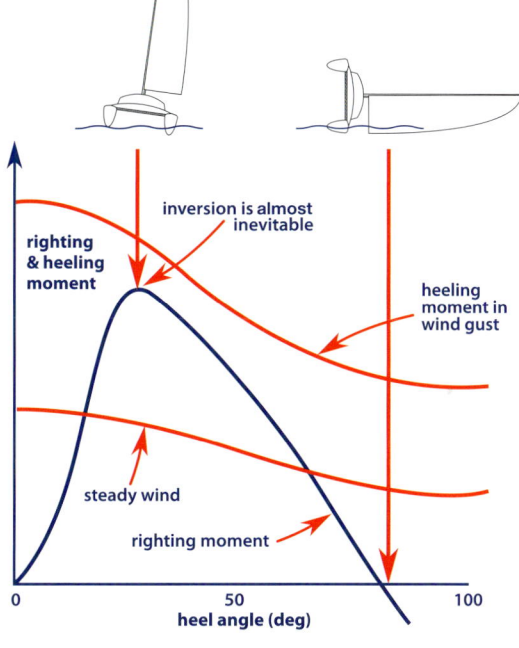

ANNEX B - MAXIMUM SAFE HEEL ANGLE TO PREVENT DOWNFLOODING IN GUSTS

Monohull sailing yachts are vulnerable to downflooding when heeled by a sudden gust of wind. By the application of a wind heeling force curve and the righting curve for a given yacht it is possible to determine a safe heel angle for normal sailing that will avoid downflooding in gusts.

On the yacht's righting moment curve (**RM** curve) (see page 17) draw a vertical line at the downflooding angle or 60° if this is less.

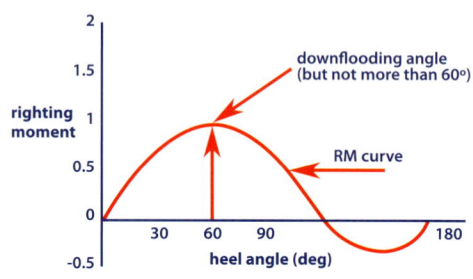

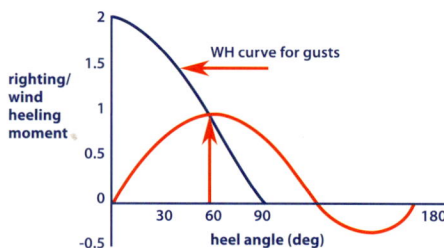

Superimpose a **WIND HEELING CURVE** (**WH** curve) on the **RM** curve so that the **WH** curve crosses the vertical line at its intersection with the **RM** curve. **WH** moment varies as

$[\cos(\text{heel angle})]^{1.3}$

It is known that in a gust the heeling moment is up to twice that of steady wind. So if we assume that the wind heeling line we have superimposed on the **RM** curve represents a gust, then a similar **WH** curve but half the height will represent the steady wind heeling moment.

The right hand end of both **WH** curves must be 0 at 90°. Draw the **WH** curve for steady wind from this point back to the left until it crosses the **RM** curve.

The angle of this intersection will represent a safe angle of heel. Keep to or below this and, even in a gust (though not a squall) the yacht should never reach the downflooding angle.

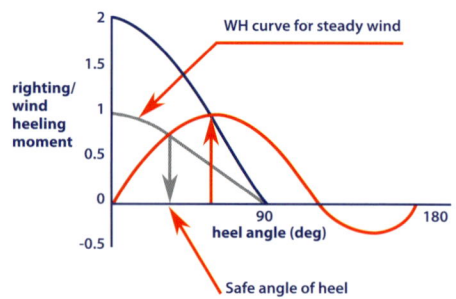

GLOSSARY OF TERMS   8

Angle of Vanishing Stability (AVS)	The angle of heel at which, in calm water, a boat's Stability continues to an inversion rather than returning to the upright.
Ballast ratio	The ratio of the fixed ballast mass to the total mass of the boat expressed as a percentage.
Buoyancy	The upwards force produced when a body is partially or completely immersed in water.
Capsize	When a boat is heeled to any angle from which it cannot recover without assistance.
Centre of Buoyancy (CB)	Geometric centre of that part of the hull of a boat that is below the waterline at any instant.
Centre of Gravity (CG)	Effective centre of the weight of all the elements comprising a loaded boat, including hull, ballast, masts, engine(s), crew and stores.
Design Category	One of four categories defined in the Recreational Craft Directive.
Displacement	The weight of water displaced by a floating object.
Downflooding	Flooding through openings that are normally above the calm water level.
Flooding	When a boat slowly fills with water, e.g. through submerged downflooding openings, or through leaks of fittings below the waterline.
Flotation	Means of providing buoyancy in a boat after swamping or flooding, e.g. by means of air tanks, air bags or foam material.
Inversion	When a boat turns completely upside down.
Knockdown	When a sailing boat is heeled until the masthead enters the water.
Righting Lever (GZ)	The distance in the horizontal plane between the lines of action of the craft weight and buoyancy.
Righting Moment (RM)	The moment tending to return a boat to the upright, which is the product of the Righting Lever and the Weight of the boat.
Significant Wave Height	The mean height of the highest one third of waves, as measured at any fixed point in a wave system, measured from crest to trough.
Swamping	When a boat is rapidly filled with water from above, e.g. by waves.
Weight	The weight of an object, in kilograms or tonnes.

9 FURTHER READING

Stability Guidance Booklet for Small Commercial Sailing/Motor Vessels *MCA*

Introduction to Naval Architecture B.Baxter *Warsash Nautical Bookshop*

Principles of Yacht Design L.Larsson & R.Eliasson *Adlard Coles Ltd*

Small Craft - Stability and Buoyancy Assessment and Categorization *ISO 12217*

INDEX 10

Angle of Vanishing Stability (AVS)
    8, 17, 28, 32, 33
Archimedes   6
bow steering/diving   22
broaching   12, 14, 17, 21
buoyancy   6-7
    centre of (CB)   8, 28
    hazards   7

cabin motor boats, offshore and coastal   21
capsize, causes   9
cartwheeling   19
catamarans, offshore and coastal sailing
    19, 33
catamarans, small sailing   15
Centre of Buoyancy (CB)   8, 28
Centre of Gravity (CG)   8, 28, 29
    finding (inclining experiment)   30
chine-walking   22
coastal cabin motor boats   21
coastal monohull sailing boats   17-18, 32
coastal multihull sailing boats   19, 33

dayboats, sailing   16
Design Categories   5
dinghies   20
dinghies, sailing   15
displacement   6
downflooding   34
drogues   14

flipping   24, 25
floating *see buoyancy*
flooding   11
free-surface effect   11, 20

handling, high speed   14
hazards common to most boats   9, 10-14
    bad loading   10, 16, 27
    breaking waves   13
    broaching in following sea   14, 17, 21
    filling with water   11
    high speed handling   14
    knockdown   14, 15, 16, 17, 19, 21
    reduction of stability   11-12
    resonant rolling   12, 17, 21
heel, angles of   29
    maximum,
      to prevent downflooding in gusts   34
heeling   19, 20
high speed handling   14
see also speed, excess
high speed power boats   22-23
hydrodynamic effects   9, 12

inclining experiment   30
inflatables   24-25
inland waterways boats   27
Inshore design category (Category C)   5
inversion   17, 19, 32, 33
ISO (International Standards Organization) 12217
(Small Craft Stability and Buoyancy Assessment
and Categorization)   5, 18

knockdown   14, 15, 16, 17, 19, 21

launches, open   20
lifeboats, RNLI, righting moment curve   31
load, excess   10, 16
load, high   10
Load, Manufacturer's Maximum Recommended   5

37

10 INDEX

load, offset	9, 10
lock walls, getting 'hung up' on	27
Manufacturer's Maximum Recommended Load	5
MCA Code of Practice for Small Commercial Vessels	18
monohull sailing boats, offshore and coastal	17-18, 32
motor boats, cabin, offshore and coastal	21
multihull sailing boats, offshore and coastal	19, 33
Ocean design category (Category A)	5
offshore cabin motor boats	21
Offshore design category (Category B)	5
offshore monohull sailing boats	17-18, 32
offshore multihull sailing boats	19, 33
openings, immersion of	7, 17, 21, 27
overloading	10, 16, 27
owner's manual	5
personal watercraft	26
pitchpoling	19
porpoising	22
power boats, high speed	22-23
Range of Positive Stability	28
Recreational Craft Directive (RCD)	5
RIBs	24-25
Righting Lever (GZ)	28
Righting Moment (RM)	28, 30, 31
Righting Moment Curve	17, 30-31, 34
rolling, resonant	12, 17, 21
Royal Ocean Racing Club	18
runabouts	20
RYA (Royal Yachting Association)	18
sailing boats, offshore and coastal monohull	17-18, 32
sailing boats, offshore and coastal multihull	19, 33
sailing catamarans, small	15
sailing dayboats	16
sailing dinghies	15
Sheltered Waters design category (Category D)	5
sinking, causes	7
speed, excess	20
see also high speed handling	
stability	8-9, 28-33
Angle of Vanishing Stability	8, 17, 28, 32, 33
angles of heel *see heel, angles of*	
hazards	9
see also hazards common to most boats	
inclining experiment	30
original, reduction in	9
Range of Positive Stability	28
reduction of	11-12
Righting Moment Curve	17, 30-31, 34
Stability Index (STIX)	18
swamping	7, 11, 15, 20, 24, 27
topweight, extra	11, 17, 21
trim, bad	10, 20, 24, 27
warps, towing	14
water, loose	11, 20
wave forces	9
wave heights	13
waves, breaking	13
wind heeling (WH) curve	34
winds, strong	9

NOTES

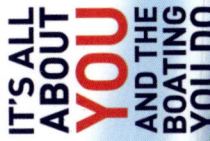

RYA MEMBERSHIP APPLICATION

Be part of it

IT'S ALL ABOUT YOU AND THE BOATING YOU DO

One of boating's biggest attractions is its freedom from rules and regulations. As an RYA member you'll play an active part in keeping it that way, as well as benefiting from free expert advice and information, plus discounts on a wide range of boating products, charts and publications.

To join the RYA, please complete the application form below and send it to The Membership Department, RYA, RYA House, Ensign Way, Hamble, Southampton, Hampshire SO31 4YA. You can also join online at www.rya.org.uk, or by phoning the membership department on +44 (0) 23 8060 4159. Whichever way you choose to apply, you can save money by paying by Direct Debit. A Direct Debit instruction is on the back of this form.

Title	Forename	Surname	Gender	Date of Birth
Applicant ❶			M/F	DD / MM / YYYY
Applicant ❷			M/F	DD / MM / YYYY
Applicant ❸			M/F	DD / MM / YYYY
Applicant ❹			M/F	DD / MM / YYYY

Address

Post Code

E-mail Applicant ❶
E-mail Applicant ❷
E-mail Applicant ❸
E-mail Applicant ❹

Home Tel   Day Time Tel   Mobile Tel

Type of membership required (Tick Box)
- Personal   Annual rate £43 or **£39 if paying by Direct Debit**
- Family*   Annual rate £63 or **£59 if paying by Direct Debit**
- Under 21   Annual rate £14 or **£11 if paying by Direct Debit**

* Family Membership: 2 adults plus any under 21s all living at the same address. *Prices valid until 31/12/2011*
One discount voucher is accepted for personal and junior memberships, and two discount vouchers are accepted for family membership.

Please number up to three boating interests in order, with number one being your principal interest
- Yacht Racing
- Personal Watercraft
- Powerboat Racing
- Yacht Cruising
- Sportboats & RIBs
- Canal Cruising
- Dinghy Racing
- Windsurfing
- River Cruising
- Dinghy Cruising
- Motor Boating

Save money by completing the Direct Debit form overleaf

IMPORTANT In order to provide you with membership benefits the details provided by you on this form and in the course of your membership will be maintained on a database. If you do not wish to receive information on member services and benefits please tick here ☐ By applying for membership of the RYA you agree to be bound by the RYA's standard terms and conditions (copies on request or at www.rya.org.uk)

Signature _____ Date DD / MM / YYYY

Source Code _____
Joining Point Code _____

GET MORE FROM YOUR BOATING — SUPPORT THE RYA

PAY BY DIRECT DEBIT – AND SAVE MONEY

Instructions to your Bank or Building Society to pay by Direct Debit

Please fill in the form and send to:
Membership Department, Royal Yachting Association, RYA House, Ensign Way, Hamble, Southampton, Hampshire SO31 4YA.

Name and full postal address of your Bank/Building Society

To the Manager _____ Bank/Building Society

Address _____

Postcode _____

Name(s) of Account Holder(s)

_____

Branch Sort Code
[ ] [ ] - [ ] [ ] - [ ] [ ]

Bank/Building Society Account Number
[ ] [ ] [ ] [ ] [ ] [ ] [ ] [ ]

Originator's Identification Number
| 9 | 5 | 5 | 2 | 1 | 3 |

RYA Membership Number (For office use only)
_____

Instructions to your Bank or Building Society

Please pay Royal Yachting Association Direct Debits from the account detailed in this instruction subject to the safeguards assured by The Direct Debit Guarantee. I understand that this instruction may remain with the Royal Yachting Association and, if so, details will be passed electronically to my Bank/Building Society.

Signature(s) _____

Date: D D / M M / Y Y Y Y

DIRECT Debit

Be part of it